Kids Can Crafts

Boondoggle

Making Bracelets With Plastic Lace

Written by
Camilla Gryski

Illustrated by
Linda Hendry

Kids Can Press Ltd.

Toronto

For my friends
in the Department of Child Life
at the Hospital for Sick Children

Kids Can Press Ltd. acknowledges with appreciation the assistance of the Canada Council and the Ontario Arts Council in the production of this book.

Canadian Cataloguing in Publication Data
Gryski, Camilla, 1948-
    Boondoggle: making bracelets with plastic lace

ISBN 1-55074-131-4

1. Bracelets — Juvenile literature.   I. Hendry, Linda.
II. Title.

TT880.G79 1993   j745.57'2   C93-093634-5

Kids Can Press Ltd.
29 Birch Ave.
Toronto, Ontario, Canada
M4V 1E2

Edited by Laurie Wark
Designed by First Image
Cover photograph by Ray Boudreau / set courtesy of L.M.S. Wood Creations Ltd.
Printed and bound in Canada by Metropole Litho Inc.

93 0 9 8 7 6 5 4 3 2 1

CONTENTS

INTRODUCTION

Plastic lace has many names. You may call it gimp, lanyard, boondoggle or just "that stuff we used at camp." It's been around for quite a while, and the techniques you use when you work with it have been around even longer. When you "boondoggle" you're in the world of ranchers and cowboys. All the different ways you braid plastic lace were originally used to braid leather thongs. Cowboys made bridles, reins, lariats and hatbands. They boondoggled — made saddle trappings out of odds and ends of leather — when there was nothing else to do on the ranch.

Today, brightly coloured plastic lace is available at hobby and craft supply stores. You can make bracelets, earrings or key chains. You can braid it long or braid it short. You can leave it plain or add beads. So when you have a little extra time, get out your plastic lace and boondoggle!

GETTING STARTED

STRAIGHTENING THE LACE

Plastic lace has a mind of its own. It bends and twists, and if it has already been used, it looks as though it has had a perm. You can straighten plastic lace by putting it in a sink of hot tap water. The lace gets soft and the twists float out. Be careful of the hot water, and do this with the help of an adult.

LEFTIES AND RIGHTIES

It is important to know how to hold each bracelet as you are making it and how to tighten the stitches. When you make some bracelets, you use both hands equally. When you make others, you hold the bracelet with one hand and do most of the work with the other. Righties will probably be comfortable holding with the left hand and doing all the looping and weaving with the right. For lefties, it's the other way around. The instructions will usually say "with one hand do this … with the other do that."

MEASURING YOUR LACE

You measure different lengths of lace for each kind of bracelet. You don't want to waste lace, and you don't want to run out before your bracelet is finished. Wrists are not all the same size, so you must find your personal wrist measurement.

Take a piece of lace and loosely wrap it once around your wrist — it should feel comfortable, like a bracelet. Now trim the lace and stretch it out to see how long it is. You use this wrist measurement to figure out how long the pieces of lace must be to make each bracelet.

UNTWISTING TWISTS

Because plastic lace has a front and a back, you will spend some time untwisting the twists in loops. A stitch that has a twist in one of the laces will not tighten properly, and your bracelet will look bumpy and uneven. But don't worry — you'll soon learn how to keep the laces flat as you work with them.

BEGINNINGS AND ENDINGS

Some bracelets begin with an overhand knot tied near the end of the laces.
Other bracelets begin with a loop and an overhand knot.
The knot gives you something to hang on to as you make those
tricky first stitches. When you have a loop, it becomes part of the fastening.

To tie an overhand knot without a loop:

1. Put the laces together.

2. Hold the laces with one hand and the ends with the other.

3. Wind the ends around the index finger of the hand that's holding the laces. Pinch the laces together where they cross to make a circle.

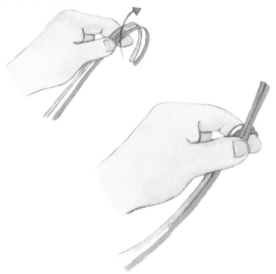

4. Slip the circle of lace off your finger. Now put the ends through the circle and pull them tight. You can also tighten the knot by holding the laces and pushing up on the knot from the bottom. To finish tightening the knot, pull on the laces one at a time.

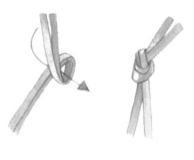

To tie an overhand knot with a loop:

1. Fold the lace so that there is a loop. Give it a little pinch at the top to make the loop flat.

2. Hold the laces in one hand and the loop in the other.

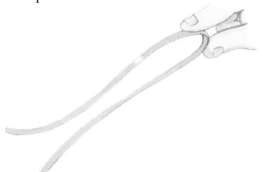

3. Wind the loop all the way around the index finger of the hand that's holding the laces. Pinch the laces together where they cross to make a circle.

4. Slip the circle of lace off your finger. Now put the free end of the loop through the circle, and pull the end tight. You can also tighten the knot by holding the laces and pushing up on the knot from the bottom. To finish tightening the knot, pull on the laces one at a time.

An overhand knot makes the most secure fastening for slippery plastic lace. When you are working with four laces, tie off two with a regular knot. Then slip one of the remaining two laces through the loop, and tie them together with an overhand knot.

THE EASY TRIANGLE BRACELET

This bracelet is quick and easy to make, but it's best to make it in one sitting. If you have to leave it, wrap a piece of sticky tape around the laces and the bracelet to stop the bracelet from untwisting.

Measure two pieces of lace. Each piece is three times your wrist measurement.

1. Put the laces together and tie an overhand knot. Leave about 8 cm (3 inches) of ends for the fastening.

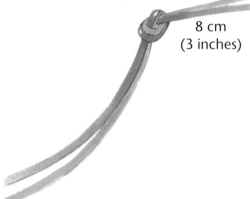

8 cm
(3 inches)

2. Turn the laces upside down, and hold the knot between the index finger and thumb of one hand. Fold lace 1 down over the knot, and hold the knot and the lace.

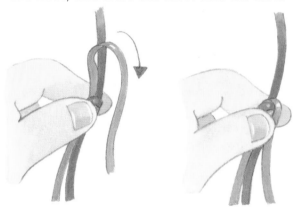

3. Fold lace 2 snugly over lace 1. Now hold lace 2 and the knot, and let go of lace 1.

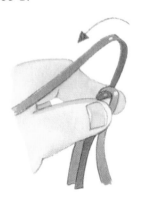

4. Fold lace 1 over lace 2, and let go of lace 2. As you make the bracelet, you always hold the bracelet and one lace with one hand. Use the other hand to fold the laces down snugly over each other.

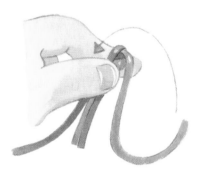

5. When the bracelet is long enough, tie an overhand knot with the laces. Trim one of the laces from each end.

6. Now tie another overhand knot with the long laces to fasten the bracelet.

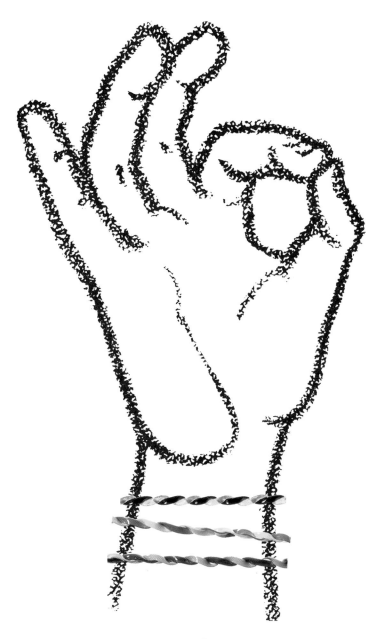

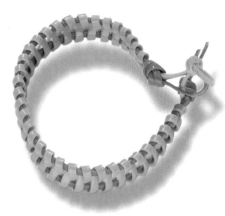

THE ZIPPER BRACELET

This bracelet looks just like a zipper when it's finished. It's easy to make and doesn't use much plastic lace.

You need two pieces of lace. The up-and-down piece of lace is five times your wrist measurement. The piece of lace that weaves back and forth to make the zipper is six times your wrist measurement.

1. Fold the up-and-down piece of lace in half. Tie an overhand knot near the top to make a loop, but leave the knot loose. Slip one end of the zipper lace through the hole in the centre of the knot. Leave an end of 8 cm (3 inches) sticking out of the top of the knot. Tighten the knot around the zipper lace.

8 cm
(3 inches)

2. Weave the zipper lace over one up-and-down lace and under the second up-and-down lace.

3. Fold the zipper lace back over the second up-and-down lace and weave it under the first up-and-down lace. Keep the lace flat. Don't let it twist. Now weave the zipper lace over and under again. Give a little tug to keep the edges of the zipper even.

4. Continue weaving the zipper lace over then under the up-and-down laces. To keep the zipper firm, hold the up-and-down laces, and push up on the zipper lace every few stitches.

5. When the bracelet is long enough, tie an overhand knot with the two up-and-down laces. Pull the knot really tight to make it small (pull on one lace at a time), then trim the ends.

6. To make the fastening, slip one end of the zipper lace through the loop, and tie an overhand knot with the two ends of the zipper lace. Trim the ends.

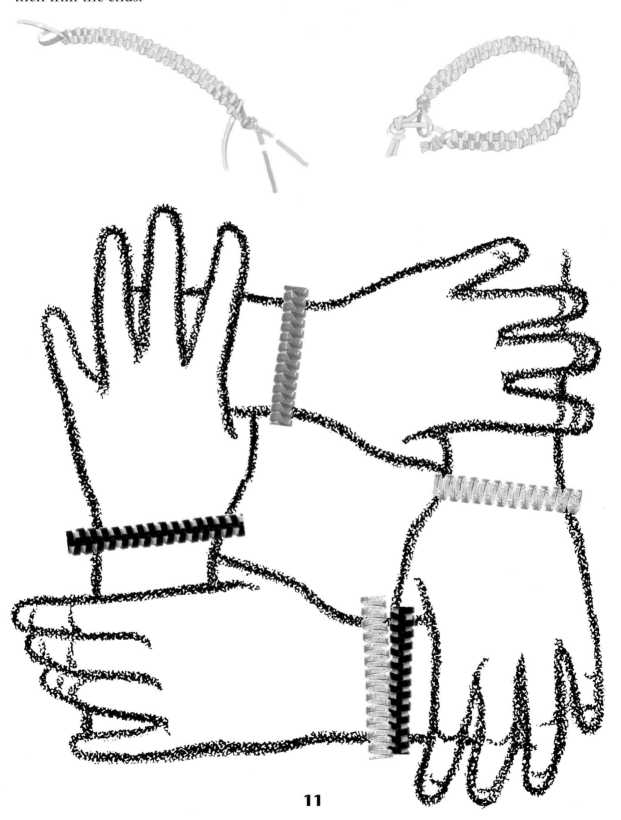

THE DOUBLE ZIPPER BRACELET

Make a wide zipper bracelet by weaving the zipper lace over and under three up-and-down laces.

You need two pieces of lace. The up-and-down piece of lace is four times your wrist measurement. The other piece of lace is eight times your wrist measurement — it makes the third up-and-down lace and is used to weave the zipper.

1. Fold the up-and-down piece of lace in half. Tie an overhand knot in it near the top to make a loop, but leave the knot loose. Slide the end of the zipper lace through the hole in the centre of the knot. Pull the lace through the knot until the end of the zipper lace is the same length as the other two up-and-down laces. Tighten the knot around the zipper lace. The third up-and-down lace can go between the other two or to one side of them.

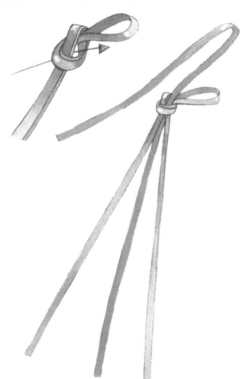

2. Weave the zipper lace under the first lace, over the second lace and under the third lace. Pull on the zipper lace to tighten it. Now fold the zipper lace back over the third lace, and weave it over, under and over the three up-and-down laces. Always keep the zipper lace flat. Don't let it twist.

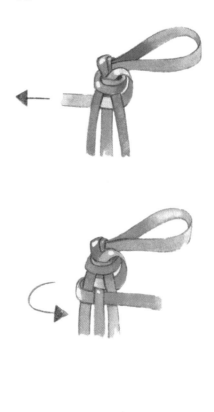

3. Fold the zipper lace over again, and weave it under, over and under the three up-and-down laces. Don't forget the little tug at the end of each stitch that keeps the edges of the zipper even. Push the stitches up on the up-and-down laces so they are snug against each other.

▲ **HINT:** As you weave each row, use one hand to hold the zipper lace at the edge of the bracelet. Use the other hand to weave the zipper lace under and over.

5. Use the other two laces to make the fastening. Slip one lace through the loop. Tie an overhand knot with the two laces. Pull it tight, then trim the ends.

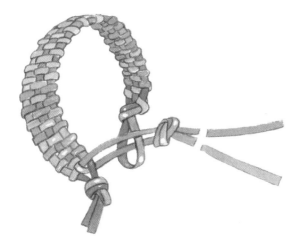

4. When the bracelet is long enough, tie an overhand knot with the two outside up-and-down laces. Pull it tight, then trim the ends.

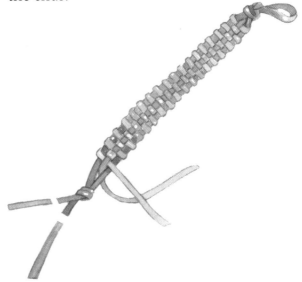

THE FLAT BRAIDED BRACELET

To make a flat braided bracelet in one colour, you need a piece of lace that is ten times the measurement of your wrist.

1. Fold the lace in half, and tie a loose overhand knot near the top to make a loop. Slip one end of the lace back up through the hole in the centre of the knot. Pull the end all the way through the knot until you make a small loop. Tighten the knot.

2. Turn the bracelet upside down and hold it by the knot. The small loop faces up. Make a loop with the other lace, and push it through the first loop. The two sides of the loop must lie flat, without any twists in the lace. Tighten the first loop around the second loop by pulling on its lace.

3. Now use this lace to make a new loop, and push it through the other loop. Tighten this other loop by pulling on its lace.

4. Continue making a loop with one lace, pushing this loop through the other loop, then tightening the other loop around it. The lace that you've just tightened always makes the next loop.

5. When your bracelet is long enough, finish it off by pulling the end of the loop all the way out. Slip one of the laces through the beginning loop, and tie an overhand knot with the two laces. Pull it tight, then trim the ends.

▲**HINT:** Flat braided bracelets have a front and a back. You are looking at the front when the side of the loop with the end of the lace is in front.

THE FLAT BRAIDED BRACELET ②COLOURS

To make a two-colour flat braided bracelet, you need two pieces of lace. Each piece is five times the measurement of your wrist.

1. Put the two laces together. Leave an end of 8 cm (3 inches) in each lace, then tie an overhand knot. Leave the knot loose, and slip the long end of one of the laces back through the hole in the centre of the knot. Pull the end all the way through the knot until you make a small loop. Tighten the knot.

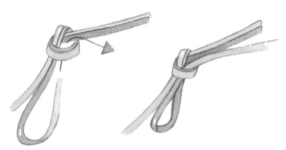

2. Turn the bracelet upside down. Make a loop with the other lace, and push it through the first loop. The two sides of the loop must lie flat, without any twists. Tighten the first loop around the second loop by pulling on its lace.

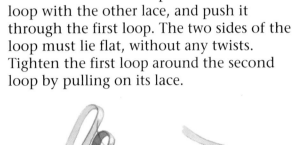
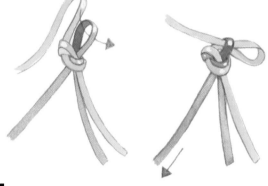

3. Continue to make a loop with one lace, push it through the other loop, and tighten the other loop around it by pulling on its lace. A loop of one colour is always pushed through the loop of the other colour.

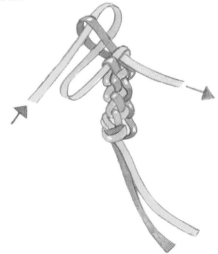

4. When the bracelet is long enough, finish it off by pulling the end of the last loop all the way out. Tie an overhand knot with the two laces of one colour — one at each end of the bracelet — and another overhand knot with the other two laces. Pull these knots tight to make them small, then trim the ends.

THE FLAT LACY BRACELET

Choose two colours of lace.
Each colour is eight times the measurement
of your wrist.

1. Fold one piece of lace in half, and tie an overhand knot in it to make a loop. Leave the knot loose, and slip the other piece of lace through the hole in the centre of the knot. Pull the lace until both ends are the same length, then tighten the knot.

2. Hold the loop and knot. Arrange the laces so that two laces of one colour are on one side and two laces of the other colour are on the other side.

3. Find the lace that sticks up out of the centre of the knot. Fold it over towards you to make a loop. Wrap the other lace of this colour clockwise (this way ↻) around the loop, and pull it tight.

4. Now make a loop and push it through the first loop. Pull the first loop tight. Congratulations, you've started the bracelet.

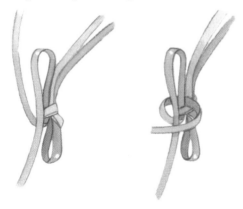

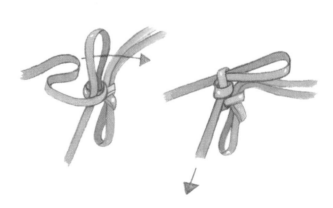

5. Make a loop in one of the laces of the other colour, push it through the loop, and tighten this loop by pulling on its lace. Now there is an upper and lower lace on each side.

6. Use the lower lace of the other colour to make the next loop. It moves across in front of the upper lace and into the loop. Make sure the lace is snug against the side of the bracelet before you tighten the loop. Always use the lower lace of the opposite colour to make the next loop.

▲ **HINT:** This bracelet has a front and a back. Always work looking at the front.

8. Use the other two laces for the fastening. Slip one end through the loop, and tie an overhand knot with both laces. Trim the ends.

7. When the bracelet is long enough, pull the end of the last loop all the way out. Tie a regular knot with two of the laces to finish them off. You can use the lower laces (one of each colour) or the two laces of one colour. Trim the ends.

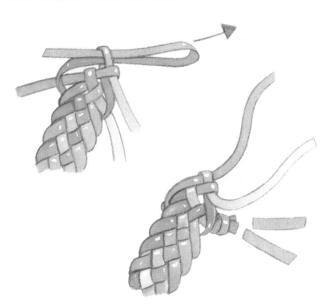

THE THREE-STRAND BRAIDED BRACELET

You can braid plastic lace using three or four strands. You must keep the lace from getting twisted and braid very tightly.

Choose three colours of lace. Each colour is three times your wrist measurement. Straighten the lace to make braiding easier.

1. Tie an overhand knot, but leave about 8 cm (3 inches) of ends. Tighten the knot by pulling on the laces one at a time.

2. It's easier to braid when your work is anchored to something, so put a safety pin through the knot and pin the bracelet to your jeans or to a cushion.

3. Number the laces in your head. Lace 1 and 2 are in your left hand. Lace 3 is in your right hand. To braid, fold lace 3 over lace 2 — it curves around lace 2 and then lies flat beside lace 1 in your left hand. It's lace 2 now. Your right hand holds the new lace 3 and the braid.

4. Fold lace 1 over lace 2. It's lace 2 now, and it lies flat beside lace 3 in your right hand. Tighten the laces.

5. Fold lace 3 over lace 2, then lace 1 over lace 2. Tighten the laces.

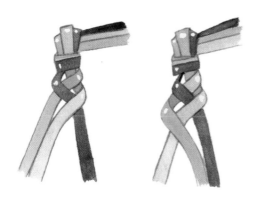

⚠ **HINT:** As you braid, you fold the lace over with one hand. The other hand holds the other two laces to stop them from coming unbraided. Keep the braid tight.

6. When the bracelet is long enough, tie an overhand knot with the laces at the end of the braid. Tighten the knot to make it small, then trim two of the three laces at each end.

7. Tie an overhand knot with the other two laces to fasten the bracelet, then trim the ends.

THE THREE-STRAND BRAIDED BRACELET

**Measure your lace.
One colour will be six times the measurement of your wrist.
The other colour will be three times your wrist measurement.**

1. Fold the longer lace in half to make a loop, then tie an overhand knot. Leave the knot loose, and slip the end of the other lace through the hole in the centre of the knot. Leave a short end so the lace doesn't slip out, then tighten the knot. Use a safety pin to anchor your work to your jeans or to a cushion.

2. Braid the bracelet as usual. When the bracelet is long enough, tie an overhand knot with the ends. Trim the short end by the loop and the other end of that colour.

3. Use the other two ends to fasten the bracelet. Put one end through the loop. Tie an overhand knot with the two ends and trim.

THE FOUR-STRAND BRAIDED BRACELET

Choose two colours of lace. Each colour is four times your wrist measurement.

1. Fold one of the laces in half to make a loop, then tie an overhand knot. Slip one of the ends of the other lace through the hole in the centre of the knot, and pull until both the ends are the same length. Tighten the knot. You have a lot to hold on to when you make this braid. You must work tightly and keep the tension even. Pin this bracelet to your jeans or to a cushion while you work on it.

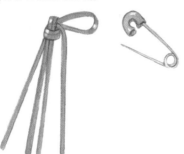

2. Arrange your laces. You can make two patterns with this braid. If you begin with one lace of each colour on each side, you will make a spiral pattern. If you put both laces of the same colour on each side, you'll make a diamond pattern.

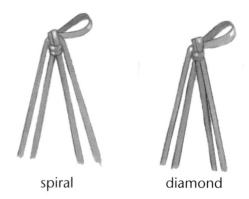

spiral   diamond

3. Number the laces in your head from left to right — 1, 2, 3 and 4. Your left hand holds laces 1 and 2. Your right hand holds laces 3 and 4. You work the braid from the right side, then from the left. Remember to keep the laces flat as you wrap them around each other. Tighten the laces of the braid after each step.

4. Lace 4 goes under 3 and 2, then wraps back around over 2. Lace 4 is now lace 3, and it lies flat beside the new lace 4.

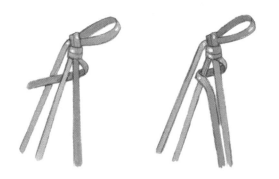

◀ HINT: Here's how your hands work together: Your right index finger nudges lace 4 behind laces 3 and 2. Lace 3 is held in the curve of the fingers of your right hand. So that lace 4 can come forward between laces 1 and 2, your left hand lets go of lace 2. Your right hand takes over and holds lace 2 with lace 3 between the index finger and thumb. You can let go of lace 1 (or keep it in the curve of your fingers) while you use your left index finger and thumb to wrap lace 4 around lace 2. Now your right hand holds the new lace 3 and the new lace 4, and your left hand holds laces 1 and 2.

5. Lace 1 goes under 2 and 3, then wraps back around 3. It's lace 2 now, and it lies flat beside the new lace 1.

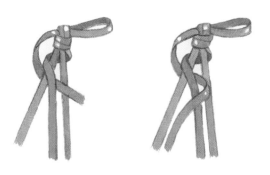

6. Now repeat the pattern. Lace 4 goes under 3 and 2 and wraps back around over 2. Lace 1 goes under 2 and under 3, then wraps back around over lace 3. Always braid under two laces and back over one lace.

7. When the bracelet is long enough, tie a regular knot with two ends of the same colour and trim them.

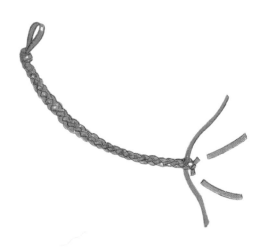

8. Slip one of the other ends through the loop, and tie an overhand knot with both of them to fasten the bracelet. Trim the ends.

THE SQUARE BRAIDED BRACELET

Choose two plastic laces that are different colours but the same weight. If one is softer than the other, you won't be able to tighten each stitch. Each colour is 12 times your wrist measurement.

1. Fold one of the laces in half, then tie an overhand knot to make a loop. Leave the knot loose, and slide the end of the other lace through the hole in the centre of the knot. Pull this lace until both ends are the same length, then tighten the knot.

2. Hold the loop and the knot upside down in one hand. Fan out the laces like the petals of a flower. The laces that made the loop and the knot are on the sides.

3. You're going to weave a square with the laces. Fold over the first lace away from you to make a loop. Hold this lace with the same hand that is holding the loop and the knot, but tuck it between your index and middle fingers.

4. Fold over the opposite lace towards you to make another loop. Hold the lace of this loop with the knot, between your index finger and thumb. You've made the sides of the square.

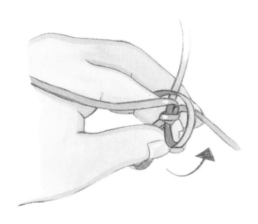

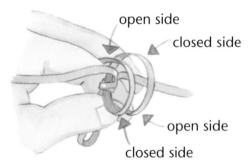

open side

closed side

open side

closed side

The other two laces weave over and under these loops. Because lefties and righties might do this differently, look carefully at the loops you are holding. Each loop has a closed side, where you folded it over, and an open side, where you are holding the lace. When you weave the top and bottom of the square, each lace must go over one loop on the open side and under the other loop on the closed side.

5. One lace weaves over a loop and under a loop to make the top of the square. The other weaves over a loop and under a loop to make the bottom of the square. Pull each lace all the way through. Make sure the laces aren't twisted.

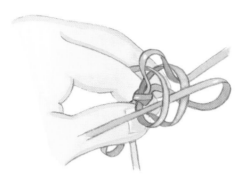

6. Here's how to tighten all four laces at the same time to make the stitch square. Hold one lace between each thumb and index finger. The other two laces are tucked in the curve between your other fingers and your palms. Now pull on the laces. Turn your work around so that the other two laces can be tightened by your index fingers and thumbs. Make the stitch as square as you can. If the stitch won't tighten, check to see if there is a twist in one of the laces.

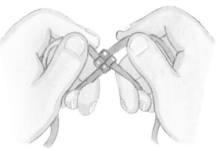

7. Continue to make side-by-side loops with the laces of one colour. Weave the other two laces over and under the loops to make the top and bottom of the square. It doesn't matter which colour you loop and which you weave. One hand always holds the bracelet, and one works with the laces.

8. When the bracelet is long enough, tie off two of the laces with a regular knot, then trim the ends.

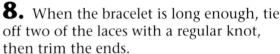

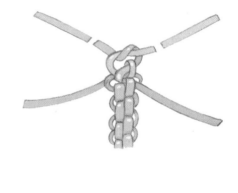

9. Use the other two laces to make the fastening. Slip one end through the loop, then use both ends to tie an overhand knot. Trim the ends.

THE ROUND BRAIDED BRACELET

Choose two colours of lace. Make sure they are the same weight. If one lace is softer than the other, it will be difficult to tighten the stitches. Each length of lace should be 12 times your wrist measurement.

1. Set up your loop and knot as you did for the square braided bracelet. Make one square stitch. Your square stitch must look exactly like the one shown here. If it doesn't, you can make it the same by doing one more square stitch.

2. Hold the bracelet so you can see the square stitch. Fold over the first lace to make a loop. It doesn't fold down opposite itself, but it moves over one place clockwise (this way ↻) on the other side of its partner lace. Make one more loop parallel to the first loop to finish the sides of the square. It also moves over one place clockwise.

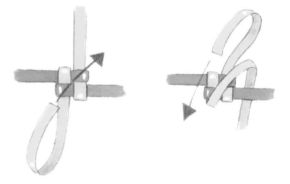

3. Hold the bracelet so that you can see the stitch underneath. The lace that made the top of the square moves over one place clockwise. Weave it over and under the loops to make the bottom of the square. Make the top of the square by weaving the last lace over a loop and under a loop. Tighten the stitch by pulling on all four laces at once.

4. Each round stitch is made the same way. Fold each lace over to make a loop, but move it over one place clockwise. When you weave the other two laces through, move each of them over one place clockwise, as well. Because the stitches turn, they make a spiral pattern. It doesn't matter which pair of laces you use for loops and which you weave through.

5. When the bracelet is long enough, tie a regular knot with one pair of laces, and trim the ends. Slip one of the other ends through the loop, and tie an overhand knot with both ends to make the fastening. Trim the ends.

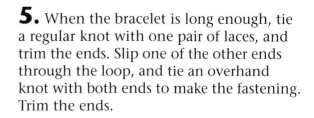

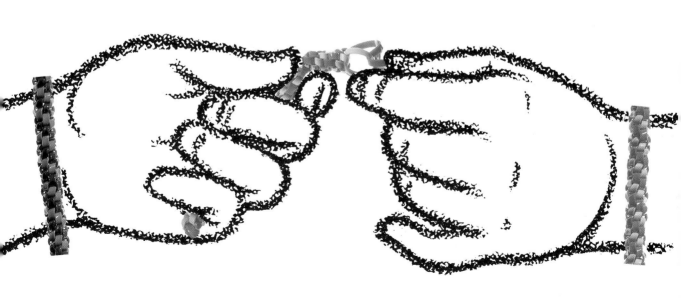

THE COBRA BRACELET

Choose two colours of plastic lace. One colour will be the core colour. You will use the other to make the cobra knots. The core lace is four times your wrist measurement. The cobra-knot colour is ten times your wrist measurement.

1. Fold the core lace in half, then tie an overhand knot to make a loop. Slip one end of the cobra lace through the hole in the centre of the knot, and pull until both the ends are the same length. Tighten the knot. The core laces are in the centre. The cobra laces are on the sides. The cobra knot has two parts — it's really a square knot. As you work, always keep the laces flat.

2. Make a loop with the cobra lace on the right. Hold the lace where it crosses in front of the core laces. The cobra lace on the left must hang down in front of the lace of this loop. Then the left cobra lace goes behind the core laces and towards you through the loop. Pull on both the ends to tighten the stitch.

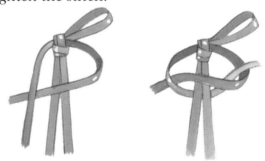

3. To finish the cobra knot, make a loop with the cobra lace on the left. Hold it where it crosses in front of the core laces. The cobra lace on the right must hang down in front of the lace of this loop. Then the right cobra lace goes behind the core laces and towards you through the loop. Pull on both the ends to tighten the stitch.

▲ HINT: Look at the last stitch you made. On the left is a loop with a lace coming out towards the front. On the right is a small loop holding a lace that is going towards the back. This backwards-facing lace is always the one that makes the next loop. If you get a twist in your bracelet, it's because you've made the loop on one side twice in a row.

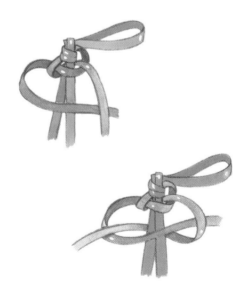

4. Continue making cobra knots, first making a loop with the lace on the right and finishing the stitch with the lace on the left, then making the loop with the lace on the left and finishing the stitch with the lace on the right.

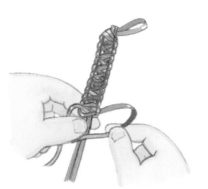

5. When your bracelet is long enough, tie a regular knot with the cobra laces to finish them off, and trim the ends.

6. Slip one of the core laces through the loop, then tie an overhand knot with both core laces to fasten the bracelet together. Trim the ends.

THE COBRA BRACELET

2 COLOURS

You can make a cobra bracelet with borders in a different colour. You measure and set up your laces in a different way, but the knotting is exactly the same.

Choose two colours of lace. Each lace is seven times your wrist measurement.

1. Fold one lace so that two wrist lengths are on one side and five wrist lengths are on the other. Now tie an overhand knot to make the loop.

2. Slip one end of the other lace through the hole in the centre of the knot. Pull it through until the end matches the short end of the knotted lace. Tighten the knot. The two short ends are the core laces. The long ends are the cobra knotting laces.

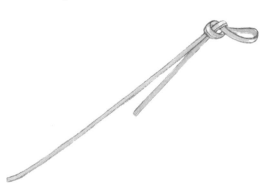

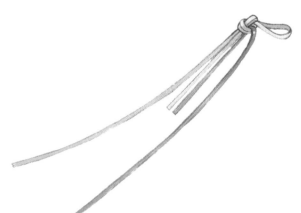

3. Knot your cobra bracelet the usual way. Because the knotting laces are different colours, the cobra knots will have borders.

▲ **HINT:** If you put this bracelet down and are not sure how to start again, look at the colour of the central part of the bracelet. The colour of the first loop you make will be the same as the colour of this stitch.

THE SPIRAL-STAIRCASE BRACELET

If you know how to do the cobra knot, you can make the spiral staircase. You just keep making the loop for the stitch on the same side, instead of first one side then the other. The stitches will spiral all by themselves.

Measure and knot the laces as you would to make a two-colour cobra bracelet. Your knotting laces will be different colours. You'll see that you make a stitch in one colour, then the other.

1. To begin the spiral, make a loop on the left side. Hold the loop where it crosses the core laces. The lace on the right must hang down in front of the lace of this loop. Then it goes behind the core laces and towards you through the loop. Pull on both laces to tighten the stitch.

2. Now make another loop on the left side, and complete the stitch. Every stitch in the bracelet is made this way. Pull each stitch tightly to keep the spiral even.

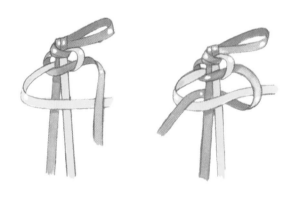

3. When the bracelet is long enough, tie a regular knot to finish off the knotting laces, and trim the ends.

4. Slip one of the core laces through the loop, and tie an overhand knot with both laces to make the fastening. Trim the ends.

⚠ **HINT:** If you always make your loop on the right side, your bracelet will spiral the other way.

MIX AND MATCH

When you know how to make different kinds of bracelets,
try mixing the patterns up to make new designs.

•Make a bracelet of square and round
braid.

•Make a square-braid checkerboard
bracelet. Move the colours by using two
round stitches. Do a block of square braid.
Do two round stitches. Now do another
block of square braid. If you're making a
black and purple bracelet, the black will be
on the purple sides and the purple will be
on the black sides when you begin your
square stitches again.

•Make a fancy cobra bracelet by adding
two or three small blocks of spiral staircase.

•Now make one up yourself …

ABOUT BEADS

When you go to buy beads, take a sample of plastic lace with you. The hole in the bead must be big enough for four strands of lace — although you can also work the bead into the bracelet by slipping just two strands through the hole and making the next stitch around the bead.

•Pony beads work well with plastic lace. The holes are usually big enough for four strands, and they come in glass as well as plastic.

•You can also make beads with modelling clay that you bake and varnish. Use a knitting needle to make the hole. Try using more than one colour to make beads that match the colours of a bracelet, or be silly and make bumblebee beads for bumblebee earrings.

•When you are putting beads into a two-colour cobra bracelet, make sure you don't turn the bracelet over as you begin again. The colour of the first loop you make will be the colour of the stitch. Of course, the bracelet will be the other colour on the back.

•Some ceramic beads have big holes. You might want to make a bracelet to show off one special bead.

•The tricky thing about adding beads is getting the bracelet started again. Pull on each lace one at a time until the bead is snug against the bracelet. If you're making a square or round braid bracelet, four strands of lace stick up out of the hole in the bead. Fan them out as you do when you begin the bracelet. It's helpful to tie a knot in one pair of laces, then use the other pair to make the loops.

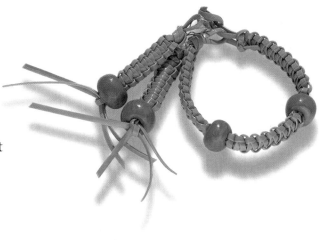

BITS AND PIECES

Key chains and earrings are great ways to use up those odd bits of plastic lace. You can also make tags to hang on zippers and pencil cases. They can be as long or as short as you like. Decorate them with beads or leave them plain.

You can finish them off with overhand knots, or you can learn this ornamental knot that looks like a crown or a turban.

1. You will need a stitch of square braid as a base for this knot. It should look exactly like the one shown here. If it doesn't, make one more square stitch. You must leave this stitch loose, as you will be feeding the ends up through the square in the centre. Each lace goes past its neighbour loop — which is the same colour — and up into the centre.

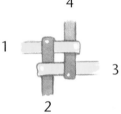

2. So, lace 1 moves counter-clockwise (this way ↺) past its neighbour loop and up into the centre of the stitch. Pull it, but don't tighten it yet. Don't worry about the other strands of lace.

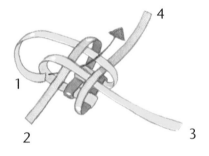

3. Lace 2 moves counter-clockwise past its neighbour loop and up into the centre of the stitch. Pull it, but don't tighten it yet.

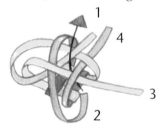

4. Lace 3 moves counter-clockwise past its neighbour loop and up into the centre of the stitch. Pull it, but don't tighten it yet.

5. Lace 4 moves counter-clockwise past its neighbour loop and up into the centre of the stitch.

6. Now tighten the knot by pulling on the laces one at a time.